MW01229720

Heavenly Prayers to Live

Inspired, Empowered, and Fulfilled Daily

(Revised)

Shallaywa Varita Collie

Foreword by Dr. Kelafo Z. Collie, M.D.

Access to the Throne Room of God: Heavenly Prayers to Live Inspired, Empowered, and Fulfilled Daily

Copyright © 2020, 2014, 2012 by Shallaywa V. Collie

Shallaywa@hotmail.com
www.shallaywa.com

ISBN: 978-0-578-65435-5

Published: by Majestic Priesthood Publication, Freeport, Grand Bahama, Bahamas.

1-242-559-2138

Dedication

To Varita and Ivan Lol Chirange Singh, may your legacy live on forever. To my husband and son, intercessors and family, this book would not exist without you. Love always and continued joy and favor from the Lord!

CONTENTS

Foreword

Ms. Shallaywa Varita Collie has coined an amazing book of prayers in *Access to the Royal Telephone*. This book captures the powerful word of the Lord from scripture and releases it into effective prayers. This book by Mrs. Collie will encourage, uplift, motivate, inspire and bring deliverance to its readers.

Shallaywa is an intense prayer intercessor who has a prophetic dimension.

She releases this book to the body of Christ and the world, in a time when the whole family needs to pray and praise. In this timely expose', Shallaywa gives the believer the enriched weapons of prayer and praise for everyday living and victory. A must read and keep for every moment of the day and season of life. I recommend you use it every day before starting your busy schedule, and watch as your day falls into perfect order. Be blessed with *Access to the Royal Throne Room of God!*

Dr. Kelafo Z. Collie, M.D. Family Medicine
Pastor,
Kingdom Apostolic Ministries International.
Freeport, Grand Bahama
www.Kamgbahamas.com
Author,
You Are My Father I am Your Son;
Understanding Kingdom Sonship
www.kelafozcollie.com

Why this Book was Written

This book was written with Colossians 3:16, ("Let the word of Christ dwell in you richly in all wisdom"), in mind, to establish a divine connection with Jesus our Lord. It is my hope that all who prays these prayers (not just read them) will find a release in some way or the other, to communicate with Christ Jesus with issues that they may be, or are, facing. It is so significant to memorize scriptures in this day and time to defend our faith and to keep ourselves motivated, especially when you do not know what to say. It is my hope that one day, when someone is faced with a situation beyond their control, they will remember a scripture or two from one of these prayers that will help them to get through. I look forward to hearing great reports!

These prayers are strictly words taken from the Holy Bible, which encourages thanksgiving to Christ Jesus, repentance for sins, comfort in times of sorrow and how to walk in line with the Lord, as a family and an individual. We are spiritual beings living in a natural realm, and so this book is to uplift, motivate and spread the word of the Lord.

(Scripture references used for prayers; King James and New King James Version)

Psalm 27

The LORD is my light and my salvation;
Whom shall I fear?
The LORD is the strength of my life;
Of whom shall I be afraid?
When the wicked, came against me
To eat up my flesh,
My enemies and foes, They stumbled and fell.
Though an army may encamp against me,
My heart shall not fear;
Though war may rise against me,
In this I will be confident.
One thing I have desired of the LORD, That will I
seek:
That I may dwell in the house of the LORD
All the days of my life,
To behold the beauty of the LORD,
and to inquire in His temple. For in the time
of trouble

He shall hide me in His pavilion;
In the secret place of His tabernacle
He shall hide me;
He shall set me high upon a rock.
And now my head shall be lifted up above
my enemies all around me;
Therefore, I will offer sacrifices of joy in His
tabernacle;
I will sing, yes, I will sing praises to the
LORD.
Hear, O LORD, when I cry with my voice!
Have mercy also upon me, and answer me.
When you said, "Seek My face,"
My heart said to you, "Your face, LORD, I
will seek."
Do not hide your face from me;
Do not turn your servant away in anger;
You have been my help;
Do not leave me nor forsake me,
O God of my salvation. When my father and
my mother forsake me,

Then the LORD will take care of me.

Teach me your way, O LORD,

And lead me in a smooth path, because of
my enemies.

Do not deliver me to the will of my
adversaries;

For false witnesses have risen against me, And
such as breathe out violence. I would have lost
heart, unless I had believed

That I would see the goodness of the LORD in the
land of the living. Wait on the LORD;

Be of good courage,

And He shall strengthen your heart; Wait, I say,
on the LORD!

(New King James Version)

Prayers to God for His Greatness

LORD You Are Holy!

Jehovah Nisi, who among the gods is like you, majestic in holiness, awesome in glory, and working wonders? I admonish everyone and everything on earth to worship you in the splendor of your Holiness. I bow down in worship; kneel before you for you are my maker.

El Shaddai, you deserve the honor, glory and the praise! Let us be separated from our flesh and be devoted like the angels who stand around the throne, elders and four living creatures, falling down on their faces worshiping you. So we can be Holy as your word speaks of holiness; holy ground, holy assemblies, a holy nation,

holy garments, a holy city, holy promises, holy men & women, holy scriptures, holy hands and a holy faith.

LORD Jesus you are highly exalted, you stretch out your right hand, and the earth swallows your enemies. Your statutes stand firm; holiness adorns your house for endless days. Your love is unfailing and your strength guides your people to your Holy dwelling.

Holy, holy, holy is the LORD Almighty! Elohim, the whole earth is full of your glory. You reign forever and ever in Jesus' name, Amen.

Scripture references

(Ps 96:9, Ps 95:6, Rev 7:1, Ex 3:5,

Ex 12:16, Ex 19:6, Ex 28:2, Neh 11:1,

Ps 105:42, 2 Pet 1:21, 1 Pet 3:5,

2 Tim 3:15, 1 Tim 2:8, Jude 20,

Is 6:1, Ps 93:5, Ex 15-11-12,

Is 6:3, Ex 18)

(Various versions of the Bible are used for clarity.)

LORD You Are Righteous!

Yahveh Tzidkenu, you are Righteous in all your ways and loving towards all you have created. Let us blow the trumpets and sound the alarm. Your way is perfect, flawless and you are a shield for all who take refuge in you. LORD, you are exalted in power; in you, justice and great righteousness exist, and we give thanks and praise because you do not oppress.

For I know that you search minds and hearts of men, bring to an end the violence of the wicked, and make the righteous secure by being a righteous judge, who expresses your wrath every day. Oh LORD, yet you have put me on the path of life and have filled me with joy in your presence!

You are Righteous, O LORD, your laws are right. Let us be exalted by your justice, so that you can continue to show yourself Holy, and know that anyone who boasts should boast in you and understand and know that you are the LORD, who exercises kindness, justice and righteousness on earth. For it is in those things you take delight.

Your righteousness is like the mighty mountains, your justice like the great deep. O Lord, you preserve both man and beast. Oh, how we praise and love you almighty and righteous One. We sing praises to your name forever. Be pleased with our worship oh, LORD, may your presence, your power, your spirit be always here with us, in Jesus' name, Amen.

Scripture references

(Ps 145:17, Ps 18:30, Ps 11:7,
Job 37:23, Ps 7:9, Ps 16:11, Ps 7:11,
Is 5:16, Jer 9:24, Ps 119:137, Ps 36:6)

Lord You Are Just!

Jesus, you are the true and living God and our everlasting King! Take Joy in what you hear and be pleased with our worship. El Roi, let it be a sweet-smelling aroma unto you. To you, LORD, who is holy and true, all power and glory is given. For it is you who opens doors no one can shut, and who shuts doors that no one can open.

LORD Jesus, we know also that it is you who have given us understanding, so that we may know Him who is true. How marvelous are your grace and mercy towards us. For your word said that if we consent and obey, we will eat the best of the land. You will not let our foot slip for you who watches over us, will not slumber nor sleep.

God, you are not a man that you should lie, or repent, what you say we believe that you will do.

You will destroy the wisdom of the wise, and the cleverness of the clever you will set aside.

For as many as are the promises of God, in you they are yes! Also, through you is our "Amen" to the glory of God. You have sealed us and given us the Spirit in our hearts as a pledge. And if we are faithless, you remain faithful, for you cannot deny yourself.

And so, Jesus we praise you, for those who suffer according to your will shall entrust their souls to a faithful Creator in doing what is right. LORD, we trust you in the name of Jesus, Amen.

Scripture references

(Jer 10:10, Rev 3:7, 1 Jn 5:20, Is 1:19,
Ps 121:3, Num 23:19, 2 Cor 1:20-21,
1 Cor 1:19, 2 Tim 2:13, 1 Pet 4:19)

Prayers of Praise to God

For Creating Me!

————o————

I will praise you, oh LORD, for I am fearfully and wonderfully made! Marvelous are your works, and my soul knows very well. You are my LORD, Maccaddeshem and the one who formed me in my mother's womb.

Hallelujah! We give you praise for we are your workmanship, created in Christ Jesus for good works, which you have prepared beforehand that we should walk in them.

Amazing are your plans for us, dear LORD. You know what they are, as your word declares; plans to prosper us and not to harm us, plans to give us hope and a future. Praises be to your name,

Hallelujah! The gifts and the calling of God are irrevocable! And you are able to make all (not just some) grace abound toward us; that we, always having all capability in all things, may flourish in every good work. For this I give you praise!

Surely LORD, you bless the righteous; you surround them with your favor as with a shield. LORD, you will be our dwelling place in all generations. You are good! I am poor and you raise me up from the dust and lifted me; who have been in need from the ash heap, to make me sit with princes and inherit a seat of honor. LORD I thank you, LORD I love you. You are my all in all, and all I need and I pray this and all things in Jesus' name, Amen.

Scripture references

(Ps 139:14, Is 44:24, Eph 2:10,
Jer 29:11, Rom 11:29, 2 Cor 9:18,
Ps 5:12, Ps 90:1-2, 1 Sam 2:8)

For Knowledge!

I thank and praise you, O God of my fathers: you have given me wisdom and power. Oh, the depth of the riches of the wisdom and knowledge of you! How unsearchable are your judgments, and your paths beyond tracing out!

Adonai, to that man who pleases you, you give wisdom, knowledge and happiness, but to the sinners you give the task of gathering and storing up wealth to hand it over to the one who pleases you! It is the spirit in a man, the breath of the Almighty that gives understanding.

Teach me wisdom in the inner most place, Almighty God, just as you gave to those four young men: knowledge and understanding of all kinds of literature and learning. For wisdom is more precious than rubies, and nothing we desire can compare with her.

Then, your peace, Shalom, which is beyond our utmost understanding, will keep guard over our hearts and thoughts, in Christ Jesus.

Change my times and seasons, according to your will, oh LORD, just as you set up kings and depose them. Give wisdom to the wise and knowledge to the discerning.

By your wisdom, you laid the earth's foundations, by your understanding you set the heavens in place; and by your knowledge, the deeps were divided.

Put your law in our minds and write it on our hearts, you are my God!

I will trust in You, LORD, with all my heart, and lean not on my own understanding; in all my ways I will acknowledge you, and you shall direct my paths in Jesus' name, Amen.

Scripture reference

(Dan 2:23, Rom 11:33, Ecc 2:26,

Job 32:8, Ps 51:6, Dan 1:17, Dan 2:21, Prov 3:19,

Prov 8:11, Phil 4:7, Jer. 31:33, Prov 3:5,6)

For His Wonderful Works!

LORD, you perform wonders that cannot be fathomed, miracles that cannot be counted. How many are your works, LORD! In wisdom you made them. All the earth is full of your creatures.

No one can probe the limits of the Almighty. How great are your works, O LORD, how profound are your thoughts! Great is the LORD and most worthy of praise!

Ah, Sovereign LORD, you have made the heavens and the earth by your great power and outstretched arm. Nothing is too hard for you. Nothing in all creation is hidden from your sight. Everything is uncovered and lay bare before your eyes; to which we must give account.

Oh LORD, I know so well that with man this is impossible, but with you all things are possible.

Every good and perfect gift is from above. Coming down from my Father of the heavenly lights, who does not change like shifting shadows. He remains the same, and His years will never end.

Great is my LORD, mighty in power; His understanding has no limit. Ah, yes, my LORD for I know that you are the one who is able to do exceedingly abundantly above all that we ask or think, according to the power that works in us!

To the only God, my Savior, be glory, majesty, power and authority, through Jesus Christ our LORD, before all ages, now and forevermore. Amen.

Scripture references

(Job 5:9, Job 11:7, Ps 92:5, Ps 104:24, Jer 32:17, Heb. 4:13, Matt 19:26,
Jam 1:17, Ps 102:27, Ps 147:5,
Jude 1:25)

For His Love!

LORD Jesus, I will fear not, for you have redeemed me, and have called me by my name. I am yours, oh LORD. Oh, how you love me! I love because you first loved me. God you are love and whoever lives in love, lives in you, and you in them. This is how love is made complete among us, so that we will have confidence on the Day of Judgment: Help us to be more like you.

Redeem my soul from the power of the grave; and receive me. For you loved the world so much that you gave your one and only Son, that whoever believes in him shall not perish but have eternal life.

I believe in the LORD Jesus Christ, save me and my household. Your word said that if I pay attention to your laws and am careful to follow them, then you will keep your covenant of love with me. LORD, love and bless me, and increase my numbers. Bless the fruit of my womb, the crops of my land. Keep me free from every disease.

I know that I live in you and you in me because you have given me of your Spirit. You, LORD, will also be a refuge for the oppressed, a refuge in times of trouble.

Hallelujah! All things work together for good to those who love the LORD; for I am called according to your purpose in Jesus' name, Amen.

Scripture references

(Is 43:1, Ps 49:15, Jn 3:16, Acts 16:31, Deut, 7:12-15, Ps 9:9, Rom 8:28)

For His Love!

El Elyon is in my midst, a mighty One who will save. You will rejoice over me with gladness; you will quiet me by your love. You will exult over me with loud singing. When my spirit faints within me, you know my way!

Oh Yes, you love your people, all your Holy ones are in your hand.

If you are for us, who can be against us? You did not spare your own Son, but gave him up for us all, how will you not also with him graciously give us all things?

When I thought, my foot slipped your steadfast love, O LORD, held me up.

When the cares of my heart are many, your consolations cheer my soul. Praises be to your name!

Oh, what love you have given to me, that I should be called a child of God!

You have multiplied, O LORD my God, your wondrous deeds and your thoughts toward me. None can compare with you! I will proclaim and tell of them, yet they are more than can be told.

For I am sure that neither death, nor life, nor angels, nor rulers, nor things present, nor things to come, nor powers, nor height, nor depth, nor anything else in all creation, will be able to separate me from the love of God in Christ Jesus my LORD, Amen!

Scripture reference

(Ps 142:3, Zeph 3:17, Deut 33:3,
Rom 8:31-32, Ps 94:18-19, 1 Jn 3:1,
Ps 40:5, Rom 8:38-39)

For the Gift of the Holy Spirit!

———— o ————

LORD, you have poured out your spirit upon me; your law is perfect, reviving the soul. How much more will you, our heavenly Father, give the Holy Spirit to those who ask you! Your love has been poured in my heart according to the riches of your glory.

You give water in the wilderness, rivers in the desert, to give drink to your chosen people, the people whom you formed for yourself that they might declare your praise! My Savior, continue to activate Your Spirit within me, that I may live. For if I live according to the flesh, I will die, but if by the Spirit, I put to death the deeds of the body.

For the Helper, the Holy Spirit, will teach me all things and bring to my remembrance all that you have said to me and give me peace. My heart will not be troubled, but I will receive power when the Holy Spirit has come upon me. I will possess the fruit of the Spirit which are love, joy, peace, patience, kindness, goodness, faithfulness, gentleness, self-control; against such things there is no law.

I recognize that the LORD is the Spirit, and where the Spirit of the LORD is, there is freedom. Thank you, LORD, in Jesus Christ's name, Amen.

Scripture reference

(Ezek 39:29, Ps 19:7, Luke 11:13,
Is 43:20-21, Ezek 37:14, Jn 14:26-27,
Acts 1:8, Gal 5:22-23, Rom 5:5,
Rom 8:13, Eph 3:16-17, 2 Cor 3:17-18)

Prayers for Families

The Mighty Women of God!

———◦———

irect my footsteps according to your word, oh LORD. Let no sin rule over me. Let me be not conform to the pattern of this world, but be transformed by the renewing of my mind. For I am to you the pleasing aroma of Christ among those who are being saved.

Let there be no condemnation for me, a woman who is in you, Jesus Christ: A woman that speaks the truth in love; doing everything without complaining, or arguing, to become blameless, and poor. For a quarrelsome or complaining woman is like a constant dripping on a raining day; complaining is thanklessness. Let there be no unwholesome words from my mouth, but only what is helpful for building others up according to their needs. That it may benefit those who listen.

Get rid of all bitterness, rage and anger, brawling and slander, along with every form of malice that is in me. I am not worthy. I will hide your word in my heart and fix my eyes on Jesus, the author and finisher of my Faith.

Clothe me with strength and honor, that I can rejoice in time to come!

For I will trust in you, Jehovah Jireh, in all my ways, and lean not to my own understanding; acknowledging you will direct my path.

Your truth shall cover my loins, your righteousness will be my breastplate, and faith my shield. My officers are peace, my walls are salvation and praises are my gates!

Create in me a virtuous wife, whose worth is far more than rubies. Let the heart of my husband safely trust me, so he will have no lack of gain. Like an apple tree among the trees of the forest, my beloved will be among the young men while I delight to sit in his shade, and his fruit shall be sweet to my taste as he praises me. He shall be known in the gates, when he sits among the elders of the land. Even my children will rise up and call me blessed.

Gird me with strength, oh Mighty One, and strengthen my arms to willingly work with my hands, and provide food for my household and bless others with my profits. For all glory and honor I give unto you who have made all things possible for me, and all that you have made is good!

Therefore, I do not run like a man aimlessly; do not fight like a man beating the air. My time, my time will be used valuably and for the works of the LORD. For the sluggard craves and gets nothing, but the desires of the diligent are fully satisfied. I myself will not be disqualified for the prize.

Let my light shine before men so that they may see may see your good works, and that my lamp does not go out by night. I can do all things through you who have strengthened me, so I will not be afraid of hard times.

Jehovah Tsidkenu, your word said that many daughters have done well, but I will excel them all. Charm is deceitful and beauty is passing, but I will fear the LORD. Whatever is true, whatever is noble, whatever is right, whatever is pure, whatever is lovely, and whatever is admirable; if anything is excellent or praiseworthy, I look for you Elohim to create it in me, in Jesus' name, Amen.

Scripture reference

(Heb 12:2-24, Phil 4:6, Eph. 4:15,
Rom 8:1, Phil 2:14-15, Prov 27:15,
Eph 4:29-32, 2 Cor 2:14-15, Ps 119,
Phil 4:8, Song 2:3, Prov 31, Prov 3:5,
Phil 4:13, I Cor 9;26-27, Prov 13:4)

For Forgiveness

Create in me a clean heart, Jehovah Gmolah, and renew a right, persevering, and steadfast spirit within me. Cast me not away from your presence, and take not your Holy Spirit from me. Restore to me the joy of your salvation and uphold me with a willing spirit.

Though my sins are like scarlet, I ask that you let them be as white as snow. Though they are red as crimson, let them be like wool. Father God, though I am not worthy, behold my affliction and my pain and forgive all my depraved thinking and doing, and forgive my debts, and help me to forgive my debtors. For if I forgive people their trespasses, their reckless and wilful sins, leaving them, letting them go, and giving up resentment, you will also forgive me.

For you, O LORD, are abundant in mercy and loving-kindness to all those who call upon you.

Oh, Father God, help me to not cover but forgive offenses as many as up to seventy times seven and seek love, instead of repeating a matter to separate even close friends.

Let me walk in the light, as Jesus is in the light, and have fellowship with one another. For the blood of Jesus purifies me from all sin. If I confess my sins, you are faithful and just and will forgive me and purify me from all unrighteousness.

Your word said that if your people, who are called by your name, shall humble themselves, pray, seek, crave, and require of necessity your face and turn from their wicked ways, then will you hear from heaven, forgive their sin, and heal their land.

LORD God, we have no power, only that which you have given us, by your blood, your spirit, and your word, hear our prayer in Jesus' name, Amen.

Scripture reference

(Ps 51: 10-12, Is 1:18, Ps 25: 18,

Ps 86: 5, Prov 17: 9, Ps 23,

Mt 18:21-22, Mt 6: 14, 2 Chr 7:14)

For a Blessed Home!

L ord, you have commanded us to obey all your statutes, to fear you, our God, for our good, that you might preserve us alive; submitting ourselves one to another in the fear of God, practicing hospitality. By, therefore, doing unto others all things that others should do unto us.

As for my household, we will rejoice in the LORD always. We will not be overcome of evil, but overcome evil with good. We shall keep the way of the LORD, to do justice and judgment. Nothing will be done through strife or vainglory; but in lowliness of mind, we will esteem each other better than ourselves.

Your word, LORD, has taught us the true meaning of love, which in itself suffers long, and is kind, does not envy, does not vaunt itself, is not puffed up, does not behave itself unseemly, seeks not its own, is not easily provoked, thinks no evil, does not rejoice in iniquity, but rejoices in the truth; bears all things, believes all things, hopes all things, endures all things and most importantly, never fails.

Father, though we may sin against heaven and against you, and be no longer worthy to be called your children, we strive to be perfect just as you are. Forgive us.

As a wife/husband I will submit myself to my own husband/wife as I do to the LORD. My husband/wife, just as Christ loved the church and gave

Himself up for her; will make me holy, cleansing me by the washing with water through the word, present me to himself/herself as a radiant church, without stain or wrinkle or any other blemish, but holy and blameless and love me as he/she loves his/her own body. And I will have the utmost respect for him/her.

In Jesus' name, my children will obey us for it is right. They will honor their father and mother so that it may go well with them and that they may enjoy a long life on the earth. Furthermore, they will submit themselves unto elders and be clothed with humility for God resist the proud, and give grace to the humble.

Through the might of our LORD Jesus Christ, we will not exasperate our children; instead, bring them up in the training and instruction of the LORD. LORD it is only in you all things are possible. I will look to you for continued guidance and I possess the faith, in Jesus' name, to do so, Amen.

Scripture reference

(Deut 6:24, Eph. 5:21, Rom 12:13, Phil 4:4, Mt 7:12, Rom 12:21, Gen 18:19, Phil 2:3, 1 Cor 13:4-8, Luke 15: 21, 1 Pet 5:5, Eph 5:22 - 6:4)

For Repentance!

———○———

Cleanse me with hyssop, and I will be clean; dear LORD. Wash me, and I will be whiter than snow. Sweep away my offenses like a cloud, my sins like the morning mist. I come to You, LORD, for only you can redeem me. There have been those who came out of great tribulation who have washed their robes and made them white in the blood of the Lamb.

Lord Jesus, you are the way, the truth, and the life. I forsake my wicked ways and evil thoughts and turn to you. Have mercy on me, oh LORD, and pardon me. To you be honor and might forever.

You gave yourself to redeem me from all wickedness, for me to gain access by faith into this grace. I rejoice in the hope of the glory of God. I believe in you!

My LORD and God, your word said that if we confess with our mouth and believe in our heart that you rose from the dead, we will be saved. May every knee bow and tongue confess that Jesus Christ is LORD!

For you are not slow in keeping your promises. You are patient not wanting anyone to perish, but everyone to come to repentance. It is a dreadful thing to fall into the hands of the living God.

The revelation waits an appointed time; it speaks of the end and will not prove false. Though it lingers, I will wait for it; it will certainly come and will not delay.

There is only one lawgiver and judge, the One who is able to save and destroy, rain on the righteous and the unrighteous.

Once I was alienated from God and was an enemy in my mind, because of my evil behavior.

For God so loved the world that he gave his one and only Son, that whoever believes in him shall not perish but have eternal life.

For you did not send your Son into the world to condemn the world, but to save the world through him in Jesus' name, Amen.

Scripture references

(Ps 51:7, Is 44:22, Rev 7:14, Jn 14:6,

Is 55:7, 1 Tim 6:16, Titus 2:14, Rom 5:2, Acts 16:31, Rom 10:9, Phil 2:11,

2 Pet 3:9, Hab 2:3, Heb 10:31, Jam 4:12, Mt 5:45, Col 1:21, Jn 3:16, Jn 3:17)

For Finances!

———○———

Dear LORD, I thank you that through wisdom a house is built, by understanding it is established, and by knowledge the rooms shall be filled with all precious and pleasant riches. By your divine wisdom help me to prepare my work outside and make it ready for the field. Your laws say that we shall not have in our bags differing weights, in our house differing measures, but full and just weights, and full and just measures. You are my Jehovah Jireh; I shall not want for anything! Hallelujah!

Oh LORD, allow me to be the one who deals generously and lends, and conducts my affairs with justice. Not as the poor man, he who works with a negligent hand, but to have a hand of the diligent to be rich. Woe to him who builds his house without righteousness and his upper rooms without justice.

LORD, your words says that he who is faithful in very little things is faithful also in much; and he who is unrighteous in very little thing is unrighteous also in much. But godliness actually is a means of great gain when accompanied by contentment. Open for me your good storehouse, the heavens, give rain to my land and bless all the work of my hands. Oh, mighty God let me lend to many and not borrow.

For I know too well that wealth obtained by fraud dwindles, but the one who gathers by labor increases it. Keep my life free from the love of money, so that I am content. Not withholding good from those to whom it is due, when it is in my power to do it; owing nothing to anyone except to love one another.

Likewise, my LORD and savior, help me to be true in all things with my superiors who are in Christ, according to the flesh; not with eye service, as men pleasers; but in singleness of heart, fearing you while they do the same things.

Giving up threatening, knowing that both their Master and mine is in heaven, and there is no partiality with you.

LORD, I will honor you from my wealth and from the first of all my produce. Hear my prayer, in Jesus' name, Amen.

Scripture references

(1 Tim 6:6, Prov 24:3-4, Prov 13:11, Deut 25:13-15, Prov 24:27, Ps 112:5,
Prov 10:4, Jer 22:13, Ps 23:1,
Deut 28:12, Luke 16:10, Heb 13:5,
Prov 3:27-28, Rom 13:8, Col 3:22,
Eph 6:9, Prov 3:9-10)

Lead Me, Guide Me.
I Need Your Strength!

LORD Jesus, I do not fear, for you are with me; I am not dismayed, for you are my God who will strengthen and help me; and uphold me with your righteous right hand.

So, I say with confidence, "The LORD is my helper; I will not be afraid. What can mere mortals and the cares of this life do to me?"

In times of sorrow, death, decision and despair, you will keep me in perfect peace. My mind will be steadfast because I trust in you. Jehovah Shalom, you will not make me anxious about anything, but in every situation, by prayer and petition, with thanksgiving, you will hear my request and your peace, which transcends all understanding, will guard my heart and my mind in Christ Jesus!

Your Holy Spirit is my helper. In the times of my weakness when I do not know what to pray for, He himself will intercede for me through wordless groans.

And I know that all things work for the good of those, who love you, who have been called according to your purpose.

Blessed is the one who perseveres under trial and do not make light of the LORD"s discipline, do not lose heart when He rebukes, because the LORD disciplines the one He loves, and He chastens everyone He accepts as his son.

Therefore, my feeble arms and weak knees will be strengthened. I will be careful that I do not fall. No temptation will overtake me. LORD you will not put more on me than I can bear, in Jesus' name, Amen.

Scripture references

(Heb 12:12, Is 41:10, Heb 5-6, Is 26:3, Phil 4:6,

Rom 8:26, 1 Cor 10:6,

Rom 8:28, Jam 1:12, Heb 12:5-6,

1 Cor 10:12-13)

Prayers for Warfare

Jehovah Rohi, by your divine power, you have given me everything I need for living a godly life. I war to receive all of this by coming to know you, the one who called me to yourself by means of your marvelous glory and excellence! Make my deserts like Eden, unleash your wrath into the hands of my tormentors, and let them release unto me all the wealth that belongs to me.

Jehovah Gibbor, contend, O LORD, with those who contend with me, fight against those who fight against me. Take up shield and buckler; arise and come to my aid. Brandish spear and javelin against those who pursue me. They make their tongues as sharp as a serpent's. The poison of vipers is on their lips. But your word is like fire, living and active and sharper than any double-edged sword. Penetrate even to divide their souls and spirits, joints and marrows. Over throw their plans and let them be persecutes by the angels of the LORD. Let them be confounded and put to shame, and brought to confusion as chaff driven by the wind.

Since they hid their net for me without cause and without cause dug a pit for me, may ruin overtake them by surprise. May the net they hid entangle them, may they fall into the pit, to their ruin. When I stumbled, they gathered in glee; assailants gathered against me without my knowledge. They slandered me without ceasing. Like the ungodly they maliciously mocked and they gnashed their teeth at me.

In the name of Jesus, I come against and dismantle every idle word spoken contrary to your original plans and purposes for my life; every curse, witchcraft prayer, and ill wishes. Put a hook in their nose and numb their tongues. Though they use their actions, thoughts and deeds to destroy me; let the heavens bow down with divine judgment to scatter them. I will not lose my property, possession, what belongs to me, due to their relentless desires for my destruction. The weapons I fight with are not the weapons of the world but divine power to demolish strongholds. LORD Jesus I pray that you fulfil the counsel of your messenger.

Release divine ambush on the camp of your enemies that surround me as you did with Balaam for you are the same yesterday, today and tomorrow. The devil will not perforate my destiny; associates and my family, and calling and use them for evil. Not a word from their mouth will be wickedness, their heart will not be filled with malice and their throats will not be an open grave. Overthrow any sabotage, rebuke and dismantle their very existence at once. The devil is defeated and you are exalted.

I declare that your light has come into the world, but some people love darkness instead of light. Everyone who does evil hates the light, and will not come into the light for fear that their deeds will be exposed. But whoever lives by the truth comes into the light, so that it may be seen plainly that what they have done has been done in the sight of God.

I will not be afraid of those who kill the body but cannot kill the soul.

But the cowardly, the unbelieving, the vile, the murderers, the sexually immoral, those who practice magic arts, the idolaters and all liars they will be consigned to the fiery lake of burning sulphur and our "God is a consuming fire."

Gird your sword upon your side, O mighty one; clothe yourself with splendor and majesty. For you will grant that the enemies who rise up against me be defeated. They will come at me from one direction but flee from me in seven.

You prepare a table before me in the presence of my enemies. I'm persecuted, but not forsaken. Cast down, but not destroyed. I am the head and not the tail. I'm a vessel full of power, and I've got the seal of the LORD! I decree and declare that I am blessed in the city, and in the field, going in and coming out. Greater is He that is within me that He that is in the world.

LORD Jesus, I thank you for being my Jehovah Shammah, I come against all back lash in your name and bind them up through your blood and your Holy Spirit, in Jesus' name, Amen.

Scripture references

(2 Pet 1:3, Ecc 2:26, Ps 140:3, Heb 4:12, Ps 35, Job 21:18, Is 17:13, Ps 135:1-3,

Is 37, 2 Kings 2, Is 44, Num 22:31,

Ps 5:9, Jn 3:19-21, Mt 10:28, Rev 21:8, Heb 12:29,

Ps 45:3, Deut 28:7, 1 Jn 4:4, Ps 23:5, 2 Cor 4:7-10)

If they are prophets, and if the word
of the LORD is with them, then let
them intercede with the LORD of hosts.

— Jeremiah 27:18

Made in the USA
Columbia, SC
08 November 2024

45703186R00035